T

know your pet

BUDGIES

Anna and Michael Sproule

Know Your Pet

Cats
Dogs
Hamsters
Gerbils
Budgies

Rabbits
Hamsters
Aquarium Fish
Guinea pigs
Mice and Rats

First published in 1988 by
Wayland (Publishers) Limited,
61 Western Road, Hove,
East Sussex, BN3 1JD, England.

British Library Cataloguing in Publication Data

Sproule, Anna and Michael
  Budgerigars. — (Know your pet).
  1. Pets: Budgerigars
  I. Title   II. Sproule, Michael
  III. Linden, Artists   IV. Series
  636.6'894

ISBN 1-85210-373-6

Designed and produced by BLA Publishing
Limited, East Grinstead, Sussex, England.

A member of the Ling Kee Group
LONDON · HONG KONG · TAIPEI · SINGAPORE · NEW YORK

Editorial planning by Jollands Editions
Colour origination by Chris Willcock Reproductions
Illustrations by Steve Lings/Linden Artists; Mick
Loates/Linden Artists; and Jane Pickering/
Linden Artists
Printed in Spain by PRINTEKSA - Bilbao

Photographic credits

t = top, b = bottom, l = left, r = right

cover: Trevor Hill

8, 9t, 9b Trevor Hill; 10 M.K. and I.M. Morcombe/
NHPA; 11t Trevor Hill; 11b Douglas Dickens/NHPA;
12 British Museum/Natural History Museum; 13 Tony
Hamblin/ARPS; 15, 16, 17, 18, 19, 20, 21t, 21b, 22
Trevor Hill; 23t L.H. Newman/NHPA; 23b, 24, 25, 26t,
26b, 27, 28t Trevor Hill; 28b, 29t Tony Hamblin/ARPS;
29b Trevor Hill; 30 Tony Hamblin/ARPS; 31t, 31b, 32,
33, 34t Trevor Hill; 34b Tony Hamblin/ARPS; 35, 36,
37t, 37b Trevor Hill; 38, 39, 40t, 40b, 41 Tony
Hamblin/ARPS; 42, 43 Trevor Hill

The photographers and the Publishers would like to
thank Pets Paradise, East Grinstead, Southern
Avaries, the South Eastern Budgerigar Club and the
families and their budgies who participated in the
photography for this book.

**Cover: These two budgerigars are both
males. You can tell a budgie's sex by
the colour of its cere — the skin at the
base of the beak. All adult males have
blue ceres as seen in the picture.**

**Title page: There are over 100 different colour
varieties of budgerigar. The two
birds in the picture are a Pied
variety and a Grey wing Green.**

Contents

Note to the Reader

In this book there are some words in the text which are printed in **bold** type. This shows that the word is listed in the glossary on page 44. The glossary gives a brief explanation of words which may be new to you.

Introduction

Budgerigars are popular pets, especially with people whose homes are too small for a larger pet such as a cat or a dog. They are cheerful, colourful birds, always ready to play a game or learn a new trick. They cost little to keep.

Budgerigars usually live for about five years, but some live much longer. Before you decide to keep one, remember that you must be prepared to look after it for the rest of its life. Caring for budgerigars does not take up a great amount of time, but they need some attention from you every day. If you really want to know your budgerigar and give it a good life, you will need to spend time playing with it and talking to it.

Budgerigars as companions

The budgerigar's best-known trick is talking, and you may be able to teach your pet to speak. But you will need to be very patient, repeating the same word over and over again.

▼ This female budgie is only seven weeks old. She is being trained by her owner to be finger tame. This variety is called an Opaline Violet.

► Half the fun of owning a pair of budgerigars is being able to watch them as they play together in their cage. Budgerigars are active most of the time, provided they are healthy and happy.

▼ An outdoor aviary consists of a wire mesh flight enclosure attached to a bird house or shed for the budgies to roost in at night. In the flight area there are perches of different sizes and shapes. The aviary has to be escape-proof.

Like a human baby, a budgerigar will only copy words and sentences that it has heard. It cannot make up sentences of its own. Some budgerigars are more inclined to talk than others. They often pick up words by just listening to people talking to each other.

Budgerigars make good companions in other ways. They are very active in the daytime and soon learn to recognize their owners.

Keeping birds as a hobby

It is not hard to find room for a bird cage, even in the smallest home. You should choose a spot out of the way of draughts, direct sunlight, heat and air vents. Remember that sunlight moves round a room during the day.

Budgerigars, like other caged birds, are happiest if they are given a chance each day to fly freely away from the cage. If you become really interested in budgerigars, the answer is to keep several in an **aviary**. This is a bird house with a wire mesh enclosure where the birds can fly freely whenever they want to do so.

About budgerigars

The natural home of budgerigars is Australia. They are **migrating** birds, flying south to the cooler parts of Australia for the summer, and north again for the winter. They migrate to avoid very hot weather, and to find water and grass seeds.

The budgerigars that live in the wild are coloured light green on a yellow background, with black markings on the wings and throat. Light yellow and dark green varieties are sometimes seen in the wild, but the blues, greys, greens and whites you see in pet shops have all been bred in **captivity**.

▼ The wild budgerigar has a greenish body colour and the wings and back are streaked with brownish-black bars. The head is yellow and the back of the head is also streaked. The tail is blue.

▲ The toes of all budgies are zygodactyl. This means they are paired, two toes forward and two behind, for easy gripping and climbing.

▼ Wild budgerigars live in Australia. This forest of eucalyptus trees is the kind of environment they like, with water near at hand.

The parrot family

Budgerigars are members of the parrot family, of which there are more than 300 different **species**. The species vary greatly in size and in the colour of their **plumage**. The word 'budgerigar' comes from the **aborigine** people of Australia, who call these birds 'betcherrygah', meaning 'good to eat'. The smaller parrots are called parakeets, and this name is often used for budgerigars in the United States.

Like all parrots, budgerigars have claws that let them grasp branches and pick up food easily. They are called **zygodactyl** claws. Two toes point forward and two backward, giving all members of the parrot family a very strong grip. You can see this when you watch a budgerigar or a parrot on its perch in a pet shop. All parrots also have very strong beaks, which they use for climbing. They have very strong jaw muscles — as you will find out if your pet ever gives you a nip!

Breeding in the wild

As budgerigars live in a dry country their main problem is finding enough water. As soon as the dry season ends and the first rain falls, the birds begin to make their nests.

Budgerigars do not collect **material** to build nests. They will lay their eggs in any suitable spot they can find, such as a hollow tree. The hen needs to roll the eggs regularly so that the chicks grow properly inside.

Like other migrating birds, budgerigars move around in large flocks. The young birds must grow up quickly so that they can join in the long migration flight. The male birds help the females to feed the chicks. At about six weeks the young birds can fly and are ready to migrate with their parents.

The first pet budgerigars

The first settlers from Europe arrived in Australia about 200 years ago. Among the early visitors to Australia there were scientists and explorers eager to learn about the strange birds and **mammals** described by the settlers. One of these visitors was the **ornithologist** John Gould who wrote about budgerigars in his beautifully illustrated book, *The Birds of Australia*. When he returned to Britain in 1840, Gould took with him a male and female budgerigar, and these two birds survived the long sea journey.

Popular pets

John Gould had a sister, whose husband was also interested in birds. He used John Gould's pair of budgerigars for breeding. The friendly, brightly-coloured budgerigar soon became a popular pet, and by 1880 hundreds of thousands of these birds were being kept all over Europe. Not long after, they had become just as popular in North America.

◀ This drawing of an old and a young bird feeding on grass by John Gould is typical of those appearing in his book *The Birds of Australia*. Although John Gould brought the first pair of wild budgerigars to Britain from Australia, it was his brother-in-law, Charles Coxen, who reared the first budgerigars in captivity.

▲ Yellow budgerigars are sometimes seen in the wild, but this mutation is rare. In the 1870s, European breeders succeeded in mating yellows and breeding from them. These were to be the first of the new colour varieties.

New colour varieties

At first, the budgerigars that people kept as pets were light green in colour. This is the **dominant** colour and most budgerigars in the wild are light green. Then breeders learned that all-yellow and dark green varieties were sometimes to be seen in the wild. They became interested in breeding from these unusual colours. By mating a yellow cock with a yellow hen, the first all-yellows to be bred in captivity were hatched in Belgium in 1872.

As the breeders became more skilful, many other colour varieties appeared, including blue, white and mauve. Now there are over 100 colour varieties, in almost all colours except red. There was great excitement some years ago, when someone claimed to have bred a red budgerigar — but its feathers turned out to have been dyed!

In Britain today, budgerigars are the third most popular pets after dogs and cats. Over one million homes have at least one bird.

The points of the budgerigar

Budgerigars bred in captivity are sightly larger than those in the wild. They usually weigh between 40 and 50 g, and the males tend to be slightly larger than female birds. An **adult** bird should be 20 cm long from the crown (the top of its head) to the tip of the tail, and about 22.5 cm if it is to be shown.

In an adult bird, the colour of the cere — the skin at the base of the beak — is important. The male cere is blue, and the female cere is brown. The beak, or mandible, should be set well into the face and not stick out too far. It should not be damaged or overgrown. The eyes should be clear and bright. Seen from the side, they should be in the centre of the head. The eye colours differ with the colour varieties and are part of the standards for each variety. The legs and feet should be straight and firm. The toes and claws must grip the perch firmly and evenly. The claws should not be overgrown.

eye

cere

beak

toe

claw

The different parts of the budgerigar's body are called the points. Breeders pay great attention to these as budgerigar societies lay down **standards** for the points of good specimens. Even if you do not plan to show your budgie or breed from it, it is a good idea to remember some of these standards. Then, when you buy a bird, you can check that you are buying a good specimen.

On its perch, a budgerigar should be steady, leaning forward slightly. The line of its back should curve slightly outwards from the back of the skull to the end of the tail feathers. The front of the bird's body should curve evenly from the throat downwards. For showing or breeding birds, the number and size of the throat spots, sometimes called the 'necklace', are very important. There should be six of them, evenly spaced and equal in size, the outer two being partly covered by the cheek patches. The wings should be set neatly to the side of the body and not crossed.

▲ This Grey Yellow cock is perfectly balanced. You can see how the budgerigar uses its claws to grip its perch evenly and frimly.

▼ The wings of a bird take the place of the forelimbs of other animals, or the arms in the case of humans. The feathers are all attached to muscles.

One bird or two?

Birds that are kept in an aviary live more like they do in the wild than if they are caged. But many people have no room for an aviary, and do not want to keep a large number of birds. The answer for most people is to keep a cage in the home, but this raises another question. Should they keep one bird or two?

Keeping one bird

Some people think that it is cruel to keep one budgerigar on its own, since in the wild they live in flocks. Others say that most birds kept on their own appear to be cheerful and active, and this would not happen if they were unhappy.

One thing is certain. If you decide to keep one bird, you must make sure that it has plenty of human company and care. It will be lonely and may fall ill, if left alone for a long time

▼ You should not keep one bird on its own in a cage unless you are able to spend a large amount of time with it. Training your pet to talk is one way of giving it your time and companionship.

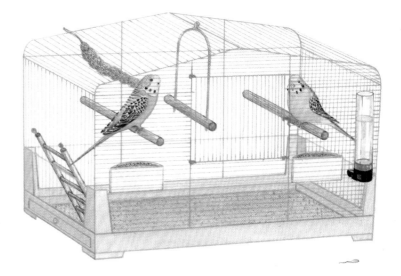

▶ Two budgies can keep each other company and will find plenty to do if you can give them swings, bells and ladders to play with.

▼ Most people say that if you keep two budgies they should be of the same age. But these two males, one young and one old, seem to be able to get on with each other quite well.

during the day. If there is no one at home in the daytime it is kinder to keep two birds as companions. If you have to go out for a short time, a radio switched to a talk programme will stop a bird from feeling lonely.

A budgerigar that lives alone will **bond** to its owner. A bond is a kind of friendship when a pet recognizes and responds to its owner. To create this bond, you need to spend time with a pet, and this often means giving up something else you may want to do. Your reward is that a budgerigar kept on its own can often be trained to talk. Two birds kept together will entertain each other and will not be interested in talking.

Keeping two birds

If you decide to keep two birds, you must make up your mind from the start. Should you bring in a second bird when you already have one, they may fight each other. You should buy two birds of the same age so that they live together as long as possible. You can keep two males or two females together, or, if you want to breed, keep a male and a female.

At home in a cage

Pet budgerigars kept in a cage will spend almost all their lives in it. You should therefore buy a cage as large as you can afford and have room for in your home. The smallest size for two birds is about 100 cm by 60 cm and 75 cm high. For one bird, the cage can be slightly smaller.

Cages

Choose a cage with panels of glass about 10 cm up from the bottom of each side. This will stop loose feathers, **husks** and droppings from going on the floor. Remember that budgies like company, so place the cage in a room where there are people most of the time. Make sure that it is away from draughts, direct heat and sunlight.

Fitting out the cage

You will need fixed containers for seed and water, also a piece of cuttlefish bone so that the birds can keep their beaks in trim. The

wooden 'tree

ladder

perch and mirror

◀ This cage is well sited in a corner, and is in a room where the budgies will have plenty of human company. The cage is out of direct sunlight throughout the day. The kitchen is not a good place for your budgies. The cooking grease in the air would be likely to harm their feathers.

bell

swing

▲ A collection of suitable toys for your budgies to play with. Make sure any toys you provide for your pets are safe for them and cannot be easily broken by their strong beaks.

cage floor will soon be covered with droppings and the husks of seeds, and will need to be kept clean. The easiest way is to use the sheets of special paper which you can buy at the pet shop. You just slide the old sheet out each day and slide in a clean one.

The cage will usually be fitted with two or three perches which may all be the same size. It is a good idea to change one or more of these for thicker pieces of wood. Then your birds will not get cramp from using the same size perch all the time.

Budgies love to play, but many owners make the mistake of filling the cage with too many toys. It is better to have only a few toys in the cage and change them from time to time. Ladders, ropes with bells and swings can all be bought quite cheaply. Make sure any toys bought are safe for your budgie. Do not let your pet have a mirror if you want it to learn to talk. It will think there is another bird in the cage, and spend its time entertaining it!

▶ Most owners advise that a cage should be covered with a thick cloth or piece of blanket in the evening.

Choosing budgerigars

Anyone who decides to keep a pet should take time and care choosing it. Most pet shops have budgerigars for sale, and there are also many breeders with aviaries. You should not find it difficult to see a large number of birds before making your choice.

Male or female?

Male budgies have quite different **characters** from females. Males are 'show-offs', always ready to learn new tricks. If you keep a male on its own, it will learn to talk more quickly than a female. For your first budgerigars, males are the best choice.

You can often buy budgerigars that have been trained, but if you want to do the training yourself you should buy a young bird about six weeks old. It is, however, difficult to tell the sex of a young budgerigar. The cere of a young male is pink, while that of a young female bird is bluish-white. But even expert breeders are

▼ You can tell the sex of a mature budgie by the colour of the cere above the beak. In this picture, the Sky Blue is a male. His cere is blue. The Lutino is a female. Her cere is a light brown colour. Lutinos are yellow in colour and have red eyes.

► You can tell that this young bird is a male. Its cere is a pink colour. The cere would have been bluish-white if it were a young female.

▼ You will have plenty of birds to choose from in a pet shop. If you do not see a pair of birds that you fancy, you can visit other pet shops. You do not have to make up your mind straight away.

sometimes not sure of a bird's sex until it is fully grown. Then the cere will have turned blue for males and brown for females.

The age of a budgerigar is easier to tell. Young birds have 'bars' of colour across their caps, or foreheads. These begin to fade at about three months. At about the same time the cere changes to its adult colour.

A good specimen

A healthy budgerigar in good condition has clean, **sleek** feathers which fall neatly into place. Avoid buying a bird that looks untidy or puffed up, or that has feathers missing. The eyes should be clear and bright, the claws should be large and well-formed, and there should be no discharge from the nostrils. The bird should be alert and interested in what is happening in and around its cage. Never buy a bird because you feel sorry for it. If it looks unhappy, it is probably not well.

Your budgerigar at home

Whether your budgerigar has come from a pet shop or a breeder, it will be used to human company. When you bring it home, leave it to settle down in its cage, but stay in the same room for a time, and talk to it so that it begins to know your voice.

Your first job is to get your pet used to being handled and to train it to become 'finger-tame'. This means that it will sit quietly on your finger without being held there. Start this training with no one else in the room. Open the cage door and slowly hold out your finger as a perch. If the bird hops on to it, let it stay for a while without moving. After you have done this a few times, move your hand out of the cage, still with the bird on it. It will panic and fly off at first, but it will soon learn that your finger is a safe place.

▶ In the wild budgerigars fly around in large flocks in their search for water. Here you can see them descending on a waterhole near Alice Springs in Australia. Wild budgies depend on flight for survival. Pet budgies have the same instincts and free flight every day is something they need.

▼ Let your budgie have time for free flight every day. Train it to fly back to you and perch on a stick held in your hand. Then you can easily put it back in the cage when its flying time is over.

Free flight

Now you can give your budgie its first free flight around the room. First, check that doors and windows are closed and that any heaters or fans are switched off. Dogs, cats and very young children should be out of the room while your budgerigar is flying free. Remove house plants or cover them as many are poisonous to birds.

When flying time is over, the bird should come back to your finger if you hold it out and call. Remember to set aside some time each day for training and playing with your pet.

Catching a budgerigar

Sometimes a budgerigar will not come to your finger when you call. There is an easy way to catch it. Wait until it perches and then use a net or cloth to pick it up gently and return it to the cage. You must make sure that you move slowly and carefully, taking care not to frighten the bird by sudden movements or noise, or it may damage itself by flying into things.

▼ If you do not want your budgie to fly away, you should hold it as shown in the picture. Support its feet with one hand and gently cup your other hand over its back.

Feeding

One of the good things about keeping a budgerigar as a pet is that feeding costs very little. The main part of a budgie's **diet** is grass seed, but it also needs oil seeds as extra **nutrients**. You can buy mixtures from the pet shop which contain all the things your pet needs for a healthy diet.

Food for your pet

It is best to buy budgerigar food in small amounts so that it is always fresh. Keep the food in a closed container so that it stays fresh and is not spoiled by flies or other pests. Always throw away any food that looks mouldy.

Budgerigars do not have 'meal times' in the way most other pets do. They eat little and often. This means that they should always have food available, and the food dish should be 'topped up' at least twice a day. Once a day the dish should be taken out, cleaned and filled with fresh food.

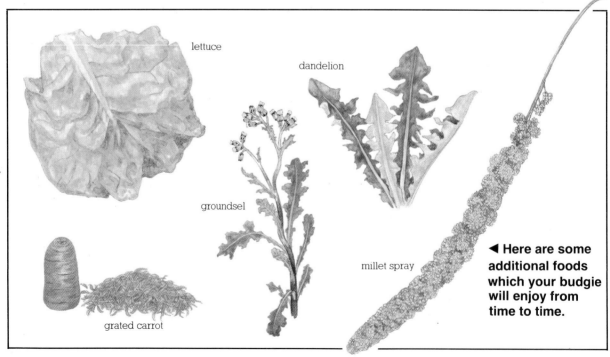

lettuce

dandelion

groundsel

grated carrot

millet spray

◀ Here are some additional foods which your budgie will enjoy from time to time.

◄ The equipment in your pet's cage should include a food bowl and a water dish. Hang up a millet spray, or a bundle of greenstuff tied in a bunch.

A good seed mixture will keep your budgie fit, but it will find life more interesting if you add other things to the diet. Seeding grass, dandelions, chickweed, groundsel and lettuce are all good food. Wash them first, and then hang them up in a bunch inside the cage. Your pet will also enjoy spray millet, which you can buy from the pet shop.

Other needs

Budgerigars do not drink much water, but fresh water should always be available. They will dip their beaks into the water and use it to groom themselves.

Birds do not have teeth. They break up food in their stomachs by grinding it with pieces of mineral block and cuttlefish bone. You can buy these at a pet shop and fix them to the sides of the cage so that they can be pecked. The bone will add **calcium** to the diet, and also keep the bird's beak in trim.

▼ All budgies need a cuttlefish 'bone' in the cage. Fix it to the side of the cage with a clip which you can buy at a pet shop. Cuttlefish helps to keep the beak in trim, and contains calcium which birds need.

Cleaning and grooming

Budgerigars keep themselves clean with no help from their owners. They will use their drinking water to groom themselves, but they also enjoy the chance of a splash now and then in a saucer of water. Let them take a bath early in the day so that they can dry off before **roosting** for the night. You will find that female birds are keener on baths than males.

Daily cleaning

You will need to set aside about ten minutes a day for the daily cleaning. Remove droppings, seed husks and uneaten greenstuff. Clean out the seed and water containers and provide fresh supplies. Loose feathers from **moulting** should also be removed.

After your pet's free flight time, check the room and furniture for any droppings. As budgerigars drink little, these are dry and, with care, can be removed without leaving a stain.

▲ The seeds which you buy for your pets have husks around each of them which the birds do not eat. These pile up and should be blown away from time to time, or your budgies may stop eating.

▼ Each day you should clean out your budgies' food and water containers and provide fresh supplies.

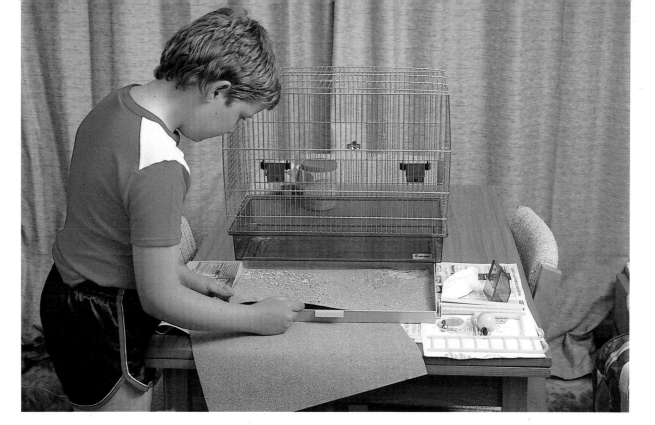

Weekly cleaning

Once a week, you will need a little more time to give the cage a thorough cleaning. Take out all the toys and other fittings, and wash them. Spend a few minutes checking all these items. Make sure there are no cracks or sharp edges. Anything that has been damaged or badly chewed should be replaced. Wipe over the cage with a slightly damp cloth or paper towel.

You can let your budgerigar enjoy free flight while you are doing all this. It is also a good time to introduce any new toys you have bought. When you put your budgie back in its cage, stay for a while and talk to it in case the clean cage seems strange to the bird.

This will give you a good chance to carry out a health check. Look at the claws and beak to see that they are not overgrown. For most of the year the feathers should be sleek, but when budgerigars moult, they may appear a little untidy and you will find old feathers on the floor of the cage.

▲ Once a week you should remove all the toys and equipment from the cage and wash each thing carefully. With some cages it is possible to use sanded paper as a bottom liner. It is a very easy job to remove the sliding floor and replace the dirty liner with a clean one. It is important to keep things clean so that your budgies remain healthy.

Health care

If you buy a healthy budgerigar, it is likely to live for five years or even longer. Some birds have been known to live for twenty years. You should always watch out for **symptoms** of sickness in your budgerigar. These signs are sleepiness, not wanting to play, puffed up feathers and letting the head fall forward.

▲ The budgie above has an overgrown beak. As a result, it must be having difficulty in eating. A visit to a vet will soon solve the problem.

◄ The bird on the left is not very well. It is listless and appears to be downcast.

Dangers to health

One of the great dangers to budgerigars is **starvation**. They cannot go for long without food, and this is why you must always make sure that there is enough in the cage. Draughts are another danger. Budgies catch cold quite easily, and this can turn into **pneumonia**. Sick budgerigars often give up eating and starve to death, so this is the time to offer your pet some special treat that you know it likes.

Food poisoning is caused by giving your bird food which has gone mouldy, or has had insect eggs laid in it. This is why you must always clean out old food each day and keep the food store covered.

▶ This is the correct way to hold a budgie when trimming its claws. Hold the toe up to the light. Then it is possible to see the blood vessels in the base of the toe, and avoid cutting into them.

28

Ailments you can see

If you check a budgie's beak each week you will soon see when it begins to grow too large. Unless it is clipped, an overgrown beak will prevent a bird from getting enough food. Clipping the beak is a job for the vet. Overgrown claws can be trimmed at home with special clippers that you can buy at the pet shop. Clip them only at the tips, and take the bird to the vet if you find this difficult.

Scaly face is a disease which makes the skin of the face and legs dry and scabby. A bird with scaly face should be separated from other birds. You can treat this ailment with a cream from the vet or pet shop.

Birds kept on their own sometimes start plucking out their own feathers. This is not caused by illness but by boredom. It is a sign that you should spend more time with your pet and put some more toys in its cage. Then it will amuse itself when you are not there.

▲ **This Sky Blue is suffering from scaly face. This ailment can be treated with a special cream which you can buy from a vet or a pet shop.**

Colour varieties

Even in the wild, not all budgerigars are exactly the same colour. They are usually light green, but some are a darker green and others are more yellow. These different colours are called **mutations**. Since budgerigars were brought to Europe, breeders have mated birds with mutations to produce budgerigars in four main colour series. This is called **selective breeding**. In each series there are three different **tones**.

The result of selective breeding is that there are now over 100 colour standards. There are four colour series: green, yellow, blue and white. The three tones in green and yellow are light, dark and olive. The tones in blues and whites are sky blue, cobalt and mauve.

By selective breeding more colour varieties have been produced with differences in the markings and eye colours. The best way to see these varieties is to visit a specialist breeder or a well-stocked aviary.

▼ For the budgerigar enthusiast, there is nothing quite so exciting as a well-stocked aviary. Here there are over 50 birds visible. They include Sky Blues and the darker Cobalts, Light and Dark Greens, Clear Whites, Yellows, Cinnamons, Mauves and Violets. There are also Pied and Opaline varieties.

▲ Pied varieties, or Variegated budgerigars as they are sometimes called, have broad bands and patches of a second colour over parts of the body.

Describing budgerigars

Each one of the 100 or more different varieties is given a name which broadly describes the colour form and pattern, and distinguishes one variety from another. You cannot as a beginner learn all these names straight away, but a few varieties are described here to help you understand what the names mean.

Opaline budgerigars are those with a different pattern of markings from the 'normal'. They are clearer on the head, and show a big 'V' of pure colour between the wings when seen from behind. The Pied varieties have bodies which are two-coloured, with the colouring broken into bands.

Albinos and Lutinos are easily recognized. The Albino is pure white with red eyes, and the Lutino is pure yellow, also with red eyes. Cinnamon budgerigars are very handsome with their warm brown markings.

► This bird is a Normal Grey cock. 'Normals' are birds with the basic patterns and markings. All Greys have black tails and silvery-grey cheek patterns.

31

Training your pet to talk

It is fun to train a budgie to talk but it takes a lot of time and patience. Remember that budgerigars do not understand what words mean. They can only **mimic** — copy — the sounds they hear. The more often they hear a sound, the sooner they will learn to mimic it.

Male birds about six weeks old are the easiest to train, once they are finger-tame. As everyone has a different voice, only one person should do the training. Children make better trainers than adults because their voices are higher.

First lessons

You will need to set aside a regular time for training each day. You should be on your own with your budgie, with no one else around, and no radio or television on.

◄ Start training your pet when it is quite young. A young bird will learn readily but first it must establish confidence with the owner. This young budgie seems to be quite content to sit on its owner's shoulder.

▲ Teaching your budgerigar to talk can be a long, slow process. The Opaline Violet in this picture is just seven weeks old. Once a bird is finger tame or happy to perch on the hand as in the picture, teaching can begin.

The first word you teach should be your budgerigar's name. This must be a short word which is easy to mimic. You may have to say it over and over again for many days before your pet starts to copy it. Remember to use the same tone of voice each time. Never show your anger if your bird does not learn. Play with it for a while and try again.

More words

Once the budgerigar has got the idea of copying the sounds you make, you can teach it more words and even short sentences. Teach one new word or sentence at a time, and go on to another only when your pet can repeat the earlier ones. If it is a good talker, you will find that it will be able to learn as many different words and sentences as you have the time to teach it.

A good mimic will not stop at copying the words you teach. You may find that your budgie will also copy other sounds it hears around the house, such as the creaking of a door, whistling and the ringing of the telephone. It may also copy other people.

Budgerigar tricks

However hard you try, there are some budgerigars that never learn to talk. But you can still have fun teaching them **acrobatics** and other tricks. Budgies love playing games, but they have to be shown what to do. Remember that birds have very small brains. They cannot think about more than one simple thing at a time. If you want to teach your pet how to play with one of its toys, take the others out of the cage.

Swings and ladders

Once your budgerigar is tame it will be interested in everything you do. Use your fingers to show it how to make a swing move, or how to climb a ladder, and it will copy you. Show you are pleased when it gets things right. Even if a budgerigar cannot learn to talk, it can obey commands, just like a dog can. Once your bird can swing on its swing or climb its ladder, you can teach it to obey you when you give the command 'Have a swing' or 'Climb the ladder'.

▲ A cage is a very small place for a budgerigar to live in. Make life more fun for your pet by training it to use a swing. Hang the swing near the centre of the cage. Show your budgie how it works by using your finger.

◄ You will find several different budgerigar toys in a pet shop. Train your pet to ring a bell, or ride on a wagon with a fitted perch.

Other tricks

There are many other tricks that you can teach your pet. You can hang a small bell from the top of the cage, and teach your bird to ring it when you give the command. Budgerigars can learn to put out a claw to 'shake hands' when told to do so. You can think up other ideas when you get to know your budgie well.

Here are some rules to remember when you are training your budgerigar to do tricks. Never play any rough games. Make sure that there is no danger of your pet hurting itself. Lastly, do not play for too long a time. Budgerigars soon tire and need a rest. Placing a cloth over the cage is a signal to the birds that it is time to sleep.

You will need to repeat a trick a number of times before your pet learns it and you will have to remind it next time you play.

▼ A budgerigar can be trained by a patient owner to 'shake hands' using one of its feet to do so.

Showing budgerigars

If you train your budgerigar to talk or to do tricks, you are teaching it to 'show off'. Training a bird for show is quite different. Show budgerigars must be used to sitting still on their perch without fuss.

The best way to find out about showing budgerigars is to join a local bird society. The pet shop or vet will be able to tell you about the societies near where you live. Budgerigar breeders and owners will be glad to give you tips on how to bring a bird to a standard good enough to show. You will also learn a lot by watching the show birds and their owners.

Preparing for a show

If you are going to show your bird, it must be trained to be steady and not show off in front of strangers. It must keep calm when it is being judged. At the show the judge may use a stick to move the bird, and it must be used to this. A pencil makes a good judging stick for training.

▶ The show budgerigars are separated into classes and each bird has a show cage to itself. Here the judge is examining a class of Lutinos. It is an expert job choosing the winner.

▼ A budgerigar show is a fascinating place for you to visit. If you are really keen to learn about budgies, you can spend hours looking at the birds and learning to recognize and name each of the varieties.

Birds are shown in standard show cages. You will have to buy one of these and let your bird get used to it. Start by putting the bird in the cage for a few minutes, and gradually extend the time to a whole day.

At the show

If you want to enter your bird for a show, you must first send for the **schedule**, or list of classes, and study it carefully. If there is anything you cannot understand, the show secretary will be able to help you. Most shows have classes for beginners.

Never show a bird that is not in perfect condition, even if this means cancelling your entry at the last minute. It is best to arrive at the show as soon as the doors open, so that your bird can settle down before the judging. You may not be allowed to watch the judging, but you can usually talk to the judges afterwards.

▼ **This Grey Green hen has been awarded first prize as 'Best in Show'. The long tail feathers of a Grey Green must be black and the body colour a mustard green.**

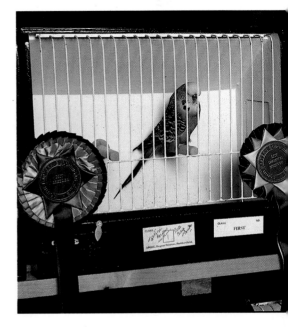

Breeding budgerigars

It is interesting to breed budgerigars, but you will need some special equipment. You must also make sure that you know of good homes for the young chicks to go to, unless you plan to keep them yourself.

The cock and hen — the breeding pair — must both be in excellent condition and health. They should match in size and age. Budgerigars can start breeding when they are ten to eleven months old, but they should not be mated when they are over four years old.

Getting started

The two pieces of equipment you will need to buy are a breeding cage and a nest box. The breeding cage should have solid sides to keep draughts out, with a wire mesh front. The nest box has a sliding side so that the inside can be inspected, and a floor with a hollow where the eggs will be laid. Budgerigars do not use nesting material but sawdust should be provided.

▼ **This shows a breeding cage with a nest box attached to it. There is an outside door to the nest box so that the breeder can examine progress from time to time. The nest box is not put in position until the breeding season begins, usually in March.**

▲ This picture shows a clutch of eggs with one newly-hatched chick. The eggs are plain white and one is laid every other day. The first egg hatches about 18 days after being laid. Five eggs in a clutch is the average, but there may be as many as ten.

The breeding season starts in spring and goes on through the summer. The cock should be put in the breeding cage first and allowed to explore it before the hen joins him. Remember that you must provide food and water for two birds. Once the hen has mated, she will eat and drink even more and you must increase the amount again.

If the cock starts to feed the hen, this is a sure sign that mating will soon take place, if it has not done so already. Sometimes a cock and hen just will not accept each other. There is nothing you can do about this except try with another cock or another hen.

The clutch

Ten days after mating, the hen will lay her first egg. From then on she will stay in the nest box almost all the time and the cock will feed her. She will go on laying eggs on **alternate** days. There are usually about four eggs in a **clutch**, but there may be eight or more. They will hatch after about 18 days.

Hatching and rearing

If you make a note of the date when the second egg is laid, and add on 18 days, you will know when to expect the chicks to hatch. Some will hatch while the hen is still sitting on the later eggs. The hen will feed the new chicks with a milky substance called crop milk.

Hatching out

Newly-hatched chicks are blind and without feathers. The feathers start to grow at about six days and are fully grown at four weeks. At about two weeks, the chicks begin to move about. Until then, they are fed by their parents. You can use the sliding door to inspect the nest box, to see that all is well. Any dead chicks must be removed.

▲ At four days old these chicks look very weak and tiny. At first, the hen feeds her young with partly digested seed and a milky liquid called crop milk.

Rearing the chicks

Around this time, you must be ready to spend a little more time caring for the birds and cleaning. The nest box can get very dirty with young chicks in it. Once the chicks are two weeks old, chicks and hen may be carefully moved so that you can clean the box. Do not wash it. Use a dry scraper and kitchen towels instead. The chicks can be put in a cardboard box while this is being done.

This will also give you the chance to check that all the chicks are healthy. You may find that their beaks and claws are caked with food or droppings. If so, use a paper towel dipped in water that is just warm, but not hot, to soften the dirt so that it can be wiped away. This is a job that needs great care.

When they are about four or five weeks old, the chicks will leave the nest and begin to look and behave like adult birds. At six weeks, they are ready to be moved to cages of their own. You can, if you wish, leave this until the whole clutch can be moved together. By this time, the hen may have laid another clutch of eggs, so you may have to prepare for a second batch of chicks!

◄ **These chicks are three weeks old. The feathers are beginning to grow. The legs and head seem very large compared with the rest of the body.**

▶ **Soon after four weeks the chicks are fully feathered and will begin to leave the nesting box. In just a few weeks a remarkable change has taken place.**

Keeping birds in an aviary

If you become really interested in keeping budgerigars, and have the time, space and money, you could keep them in an aviary instead of cages. Birds in an aviary have more freedom to fly and can live a more natural life than in a cage. You can add interest to your hobby by keeping other birds such as cockatiels and the larger finches.

The aviary

There are two parts to an aviary — the **bird house** and the flight area. The bird house must be dry and free from draughts, but it must also have a **ventilator** so that the air is kept fresh. There should be a small sliding door so that the birds can be shut in at night to roost on the perches provided. The flight area must be escape-proof. Food and water should be sheltered by a roof, and there must be plenty of perches. The flight area should be in the sun for part of the day.

▼ This aviary is home-made and yet serves the purpose quite well. The bird house has a pop hole and a sliding door which can be closed in the evening. There are also sleeping compartments in the flight area, which may be used as nesting boxes in the breeding season.

▲ This large outdoor aviary is well made with strong timber supports and a brick base for safety. You can see the double safety doors at the right of the picture. The outer door must be shut before the inner door is opened. This prevents the birds from escaping.

With adult help, you could adapt a small garden shed as the bird house, with an outside flight area made of wire mesh on wooden frames. You will need a double door so that you can enter the flight area without letting the birds escape. Most important, your birds must be safe from rats, foxes, cats and other **predators**. Some of the books listed on page 45 will tell you more about building an aviary.

Once you have built your aviary, you will need to put some toys in the flight area to keep your birds amused. As there is so much more space than in a cage, you should be able to think of some really good ideas. If you have your own aviary, you will certainly want to join a local bird society. Your vet, pet shop or the public library will help you.

Glossary

aborigines: the first people to live in a country

acrobatics: climbing and swinging skills

adult: a bird that is fully grown

alternate: with a day in between. Every other day

aviary: a home for birds where they can fly freely

bird house: a part of an aviary which can be shut up at night

bond: the understanding between one creature and another. To create that understanding or affection

calcium: a chemical needed for bone growth in animals

captivity: being kept in a cage or aviary

character: nature or type of behaviour

clutch: a batch of eggs or chicks

diet: a mixture of different food

dominant: describes the main quality or colour that is passed on

husk: the outer case of a seed

mammal: an animal that gives birth to live young which feed on the mother's milk

material: things from which something is made

migrating: moving from one place to another

mimic: to copy or imitate

moult: to lose feathers at a particular time of the year

mutation: a difference in appearance between adults and one of their young

nutrients: parts of food important for good health

ornithologist: an expert on birds

plumage: all the feathers on a bird

pneumonia: a serious lung disease with difficulty in breathing

predator: an animal that hunts and kills other animals

roost: to perch in order to sleep

schedule: a list of different classes at a show

selective breeding: breeding from a carefully chosen male and female to produce young with required looks and qualities

sleek: smooth and tidy

species: a group of animals that can breed amongst themselves

standard: rules of excellence laid down for judging

starvation: serious lack of food that may result in death

symptoms: the signs of an illness

tone: a shade of colour

ventilator: a shutter which lets stale air out of a building and fresh air in

zygodactyl: arrangement of claws in pairs, two toes pointing forward and two back, so that the claws can grip evenly and firmly

Further reading

For younger readers:

Tina Hearne, *Care for your Budgerigar*, Collins, 1985
Tina Hearne, *The Observer's Book of Pets*, Warne, 1978
Dick King-Smith, *Pets for Keeps*, Puffin Books, 1986

For older readers:

David Alderton, *Budgerigars*, Saiga Publishing, 1981
David Alderton, *Guide to Cage Birds*, Saiga Publishing, 1980
Budgies, Salamander Books, 1988
Opal Dunigan, *Training Budgerigars to talk*, TFH Publications, 1981
E.H. Hart, *Budgerigar Handbook*, Saiga Publishing, 1970
Brian Robinson, *Beginner's Guide to Budgerigars*, Paradise Press, 1985
A. Rutgers, *Budgerigars in Colour*, Blandford Press, 1983

Bird Magazine:

Cage and Aviary Birds

Useful addresses

British Veterinary Association, 7 Mansfield Street, London W1M 0AT
The Budgerigar Society, 57 St Stephens Chambers, Bank Court, Hemel Hempstead, Herts
The Pet Health Council, 418–422 Strand, London WC2R 0PL
Royal Society for the Prevention of Cruelty to Animals, The Manor House, Horsham, West Sussex RH12 1HG

Other countries:

The American Budgerigar Society Inc, 2 Farnum Road, Warwick, Rhode Island 02888
The Budgerigar and Foreign Bird Society of Canada, 17 Appian Drive, Willowdale, Ontario M2J 2P7

Index